Why Do Families Break Up?

Jane Bingham

Chicago, Illinois

© 2005 Raintree
Published by Raintree
a division of Reed Elsevier, Inc.
Chicago, Illinois
Customer Service 888-363-4266
Visit our website at www.raintreelibrary.com

Every effort has been made to trace copyright
holders of any material reproduced in this book.
Any omissions will be rectified in subsequent
printings if notice is given.

**Library of Congress Cataloging-in-Publication
Data:**
Bingham, Jane.
  Why do families break up? / Jane Bingham.
    p. cm. -- (Exploring tough issues)
Includes bibliographical references and index.
Contents: Getting along -- Daily life -- When
things go wrong -- How it
feels -- Splitting up -- Moving on.
  ISBN 0-7398-6683-4 (lib. bdg.)
  1. Divorce--Juvenile literature. 2. Broken homes--
Juvenile
literature. [1. Divorce.] I. Title. II. Series.
  HQ814.B475 2005
  306.89--dc22

2003020285

08 07 06 05 04
10 9 8 7 6 5 4 3 2 1

Printed by C&C Offset Printing Co., Ltd, China

Picture acknowledgments
The publisher would like to thank the following
for their kind permission to use their pictures:
pp. 4, 10 Topham/ImageWorks (Bob Collins); pp. 5,
6, 7, 8, 15, 22, 24, 31, 32, 34, 35, 38, 39, 44 Angela
Hampton Family Life Picture Library; pp. 9, 13, 14, 17,
23, 25, 27, 30, 42, 45 Hodder Wayland Picture Library
(Jeff Isaac Greenberg); p. 11 John Birdsall Social Issues
Photo Library; p. 12 Topham/ImageWorks
(Esbin/Anderson); pp. 16, 33 Topham/ImageWorks
(Bob Daemmrich); pp. 18, 19, 29 Topham/ImageWorks
(Nancy Richmond); p. 20 Photofusion (Emma Smith);
p. 21 Topham/ImageWorks (Eastcott/Momatiuk); p.
26, 28 Topham/ImageWorks (Michael Siluk), pp. 36,
37 Topham/ImageWorks (Monika Graff); p. 40 Skjold
Photos; p. 41 Topham/Photri; p. 43
Topham/ImageWorks (Dion Ogust).

Cover picture: Father and son in a home office.
Corbis

Contents

1. Happily Ever After?   **4**

2. Getting Along   **6**

3. When Things Go Wrong   **10**

4. How It Feels   **24**

5. Splitting Up   **32**

6. Moving On   **42**

Glossary   46
Further Information   47
Index   48

1. Happily Ever After?

A perfect start?

In the past when a couple got married everyone assumed the couple would stay together until one of them died. Divorce was very rare. Today, most people still hope that their marriage will last forever, but they also know that in many parts of the world as many as one in three couples do not stay married.

The rising divorce rate is not necessarily a sign that couples are less happy than they were in the past, or that marriages are less successful. Divorces are simply easier to obtain than they used to be, and there is less societal pressure to stay in an unhappy marriage.

▶ *Most married couples hope that they'll always be happy together.*

4

Divorce figures are rising all the time and marriages are lasting for shorter periods. Some couples may break up without too much suffering, but for many families the experience of divorce is very painful. During the time that a couple's relationship is falling apart, other members of the family suffer. After the split, some parents will not see as much of their children as they would like, and the children may no longer live with both parents.

In the past a "nuclear family" was considered the norm. A nuclear family consists of only two parents and their children. Today many other types of families are considered healthy and normal.

▲ Not all marriages last a lifetime. Breaking up can be a very lonely time for everyone involved.

FACT:
In the year 2000, experts estimated that approximately 50 percent of all marriages in the United States were likely to end in divorce, so that for every two marriages there was one divorce. In Great Britain and Australia, the figure is about 40 percent, with two in five marriages not lasting beyond 15 years. In Britain it is estimated that about 40 percent of children under the age of 18 will have parents who divorce before the child turns 18.

2. Getting Along

Making it work

At some point in their lives, many adults make the decision that they want to share their life with someone else. They may get married or decide to live together without being married. Either way, settling down together is a very big step.

Sharing your life with someone else isn't easy, but it can be very rewarding. Many couples manage to have fun together for years, enjoying the good times and helping each other through difficulties as well. No matter what happens, they manage to stay really good friends. So how do they do it?

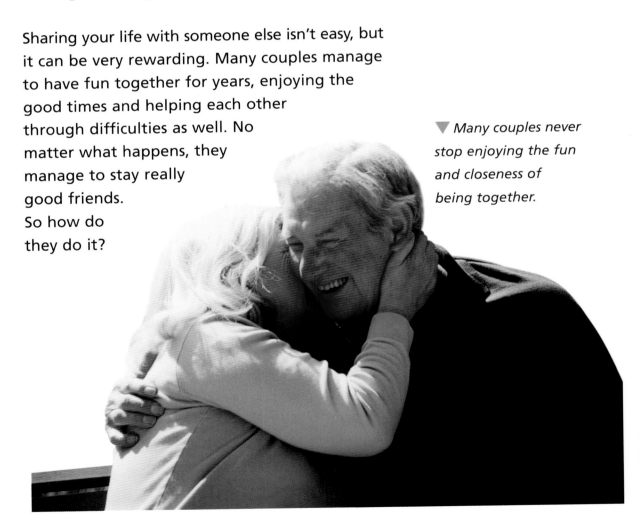

▼ Many couples never stop enjoying the fun and closeness of being together.

One thing that can make a big difference in a relationship is communication. If one partner is sad or angry, or just needs some time alone, it often helps if the couple talks about their feelings, instead of bottling everything up inside.

Living with someone every day is quite a challenge. No one can look fantastic and be in a good mood all the time, and it's important for people to be realistic about their daily life together. However well two people get along together, there will always be some things about one another that they find annoying. But talking together calmly about the things they find difficult can be helpful.

Being happy together doesn't mean that people have to spend all their time in each other's company. Everyone needs to have their own friends and "space," and the freedom to pursue their own interests. Many couples choose to spend some time apart doing something they enjoy, but this doesn't stop them from having lots of fun when they are together.

"I think of Meg as my best friend, we get along really well, and have lots of fun with our friends and the kids. But we don't spend all our free time together. I still go bicycling a lot and Meg plays in her band."

Steve, married to Meg for eighteen years, with three children

▶ *Couples don't have to spend all their time together. Sometimes it's good to do something just for you!*

Good times, bad times

In any relationship it's important to concentrate on the good things about being together. One way that couples and families can really enjoy each other's company is by making the opportunity to have some fun together every day.

Having fun can be as simple as sharing a funny story about what has happened during the day, or all getting together to watch a favorite TV show. Celebrating special occasions and going on outings and vacations all help couples and families enjoy each other's company and make them feel that they belong together.

However, life can't always be fun, and even the happiest families go through difficult times.

▲ *Family vacations are a great time for having fun together.*

Sometimes one partner may be under a lot of strain. They may be unhappy at work, or worried about money, or someone close to them may have died. When someone is unhappy and stressed, they can lose their temper easily and snap at the people around them.

At times like this, the other members of the family need to be very understanding. Even if they want to shout back, they need to think about why the person's behavior has changed and try to be sympathetic. Once a couple has gotten through a difficult period, they can look back and feel proud that they have faced the problem together. They will probably realize that this has made their relationship stronger.

Sadly some bad times go on for a very long period and it just doesn't seem possible to make things better.

▲ When someone in the family is worried or under a lot of strain, everyone else needs to be especially understanding.

case study · case study · case study · case study · case study

When Sam was 10, his family moved to a new town. His dad was very busy in his new job, and came home really tired each night. His mom couldn't find any interesting work and missed her old friends. When Sam went to bed, he heard his parents shouting. They were both unhappy and took it out on each other. For a while Sam was scared that that his parents would break up. But eventually, they decided to support each other, instead of feeling angry and alone. Gradually things got better. His dad became less stressed, his mom found a new job, and the family started having fun together again.

3. When Things Go Wrong

Different dreams

When two people get married or decide to live together, the last thing they think about is splitting up. But gradually they may discover that their life together is just not working out the way they had hoped.

▼ *It's good sometimes to be independent, but some couples discover that they want very different things out of life.*

After a couple has been together for a while, one or both of them may begin to think that they have made a mistake. They may discover that their partner is very different from the person they thought they were marrying. This sometimes happens when people get married in a hurry. Often couples in this situation try very hard to get along, but then one partner may decide that it would be better for both of them if they separated. The other partner may also agree.

case study • case study • case study • case study • case study

Leon and Martha started dating when they were sixteen and got married when they were nineteen. But by the time they were 22 they realized that they wanted very different things. Martha wanted to travel around the world, but Leon wanted to settle down and have a family. They had completely different friends and spent less and less time together. Eventually they both agreed that they should split up.

▶ *Couples who get engaged when they are young sometimes find that they grow apart as they get older.*

Sometimes couples get together when they are still very young. Then, as they grow older, they develop different interests. Eventually they realize that they no longer have very much in common.

If a couple is very unhappy together they may decide that the best thing to do is to split up. Today it's much easier to get a divorce than it was a few generations ago, and couples are not looked down on as much for breaking up.

Quarrels and arguments

Some couples agree to part without too many disagreements, but for most people there is a long and painful period of arguments before they split up. Of course, everyone has disagreements, which can be very useful for clearing the air. But when people get really angry with each other all the time it is usually a sign that they are unhappy about their lives.

▼ *When an argument starts, people can say all sorts of hurtful things to each other.*

When couples are unhappy together they can argue about almost anything: how they spend their time, what friends they see, even what shows they watch on TV. One subject that often causes arguments is money. A lot of couples disagree about how much money they should spend and what they should be spending it on. In many families one or both partners feel under a lot of pressure to earn more money. They put in long hours at work and, when they get home, they are often tired and irritable.

Sometimes one partner cannot stop criticizing the other. This can easily lead to each of them blaming the other for the things that are going wrong in their lives.

▼ *Being stuck in the middle of a fight can feel really terrible.*

In some families parents disagree about the way to bring up their children. One parent might expect the children to be very well behaved while the other is more relaxed. In these cases it can be hard for the children who are caught in the middle.

"In the months before Mom and Dad split up they were arguing every night. I used to hear them after I had gone to bed when they thought I was asleep. It made me feel terrible. I wish they'd told me more about what was going on."

Gaby, age twelve

Nobody's talking

Not everyone has arguments. Some people have different ways of coping with unhappiness. They withdraw into themselves and don't talk about what they are feeling and thinking. This can leave their partner feeling cut off and can be very difficult for the whole family. An unhappy atmosphere can build up, as if all the unsaid things are just waiting to burst out.

◀ *It can be hard to be part of a family where nobody's talking.*

Non-communication doesn't have to be silent. Sometimes people simply refuse to listen to what their partner is telling them. Whenever a topic comes up that they don't like, they rapidly change the subject.

If a couple feels that they have stopped communicating with each other, they may turn to someone else instead. This may be a friend or a relative who understands something of their situation. Sometimes this can be helpful, as the friend helps them to work out what is making them unhappy and perhaps persuades them to talk to each other about it.

"I could tell Mom and Dad weren't getting along because they just didn't talk to each other. The only person they talked to was me. I started to spend as much time out of the house as possible, just to get away from the silence."

Luke, age thirteen

However, after a long time of trying to communicate, one or both partners may decide that they simply cannot talk to each other and it would be better if they split up. Sometimes one partner may fall in love with someone else, and feel that this new person understands him or her much better than his or her partner does. Eventually the person may decide that he or she must leave his or her partner to go to live with the new person.

▶ *When a relationship has problems some couples just stop trying to communicate with each other.*

Facing difficulties

Sooner or later many families have to face challenges and problems. One partner may lose a job or become ill. The family may have to move to another part of the country, or even abroad, or a family member such as a grandparent may die. These situations put pressure on a relationship, but usually the difficulties can be overcome. However, if a couple is not getting along, the problem can make things worse and drive them farther apart.

Money worries put a great strain on families. If one partner is fired from a job or owns a business that goes bankrupt, it can be hard for his or her partner not to be angry about the difficulties that the family is having. Even in cases where no one is to blame, if one partner is laid off or simply cannot find a job, there are still problems to deal with as the family struggles to manage with less money.

▼ These workers have just learned that their factory is closing down. Losing their jobs will put a big strain on their families.

Illness can also make life difficult. If one partner becomes seriously ill, the other has to take on more responsibility. The person who is still fit and well may feel that his or her partner has been changed by the illness and doesn't seem to be the same person they married.

The death of a family member can have a shattering effect on the entire family, as each of them tries to come to terms with the loss in his or her own way. Sometimes instead of sharing their sadness, people can withdraw into themselves and become cut off from the rest of the family.

"Granny lived just around the corner from us and we used to see her every day. When she died we were all really upset, but Mom went to pieces. She couldn't stop crying and stayed in all the time. After a few weeks, Dad thought Mom ought to be getting over it, but she said she couldn't and they started to argue. It was awful, missing Granny and seeing my parents fighting all the time."

Ellie, age ten

▲ *Sometimes when a family member such as a grandparent dies, it can make everyone in the family feel very alone.*

New challenges

Moving can be an exciting new challenge, but it can also put families under a lot of pressure. There is a great deal of work involved in packing up all your possessions and settling into a new place, even if it is only around the corner. But when families have to move far away, it can be hard for everyone.

When a family moves, everyone has new things to get used to. If one or both parents are starting a new job, they may be worried about how they will cope, and the whole family will miss old friends and neighbors. At times like this, it is easy to blame a partner when things go wrong. Just when families need to support each other the most, they may feel instead that they are falling apart.

▲ *Moving can be very exciting, but it can also cause a lot of stress and lead to family arguments.*

Usually the birth of a new baby is a very happy event that brings the family closer together, but in some families, having a new baby can cause a lot of stress. Often both parents are very tired. The couple may be worried about how they will cope and concerned that there isn't enough money to go around. The other children in the family may also have problems getting used to the baby. While everyone is telling them how happy they must be, the family may actually be feeling unhappy and worried.

▲ *In addition to coping with a new baby, parents often need to reassure their other children, who can be feeling very left out.*

"After Cary was born, Alan wanted us to move again. We'd moved around the country for the last ten years as Alan took new jobs working in hotels. The kids were tired of changing schools and I was just worn out. I told him that I'd had enough this time and I was going to stay put."

Julie, mother of four, married to Alan for twelve years

Major problems

Some families have major difficulties to cope with. One or both parents may be addicted to drugs or alcohol, or there may be problems with violence in the home. Serious problems like these are hard to solve without a lot of encouragement and help, so most people benefit from the help of skilled professionals such as social workers and counselors.

▼ *Some people start drinking too much alcohol because they are feeling depressed. This can be very hard for their partners to deal with.*

Sometimes, one partner may become addicted to drugs or alcohol after a couple has been marrried for a while. Or they may already have had a problem before the couple got together. As time goes on, the problem may become increasingly serious until one partner feels that he or she just cannot cope with it anymore.

Some people repeatedly hurt and abuse their partners and even the children in the family. This is a terrifying experience for the whole family. It is very important in these situations that the victims of violence do not suffer in silence. People who are abused by violent partners should contact their local women's shelter. Even if the victim is male, the shelter can offer advice. Children should also seek out help by talking to a teacher, a doctor, or a relative. In most cases, teachers and doctors are required by law to help an abused child find support and advice. There are also toll-free phone numbers and websites that children can access if they are worried or frightened by any situation at home.

▲ If a person is being abused, it is vital that he or she find someone to help. This woman is at a home for victims of domestic violence.

FACT:
Alcohol abuse has a dramatic effect on marriage. Studies show that the divorce rate is higher in marriages where one partner drinks heavily compared to those without any alcohol problems.

Counseling can help

Sometimes couples or families who are having problems decide to see a counselor. Counselors are specially trained to recognize difficulties in relationships and to help people work through their problems.

If a couple is not communicating well, a counselor can encourage them to talk and listen to each other. Counselors can help couples to explore their problems together and work out what they really want.

Many couples find that counseling helps them to stay together. Once they start to work through their problems, they may begin to enjoy their life together again. However, others decide that they need to split up. When a couple is separating, a counselor can help them talk to each other calmly and work out the best way for them to part. This help is especially valuable when children are involved.

▲ *Counselors are trained to help couples talk about their problems and encourage them to communicate better.*

In some cases the whole family may see the counselor, and children may be encouraged to talk about their feelings. This can be very helpful, especially in families where no one is talking very much.

Often a young person may choose to see a counselor on his or her own to talk about feelings and the problems he or she is experiencing because his or her parents are splitting up. It can be a great comfort to talk to someone who has a lot of experience and who understands what you are going through.

▼ *Talking to someone about what is worrying you can be a great relief.*

Sad and angry

◀ Many young people feel sad and tearful in the early stages of a family breakup.

When the children of separating parents first realize that their mom and dad are splitting up, it is usual for them to feel a mixture of emotions. Over the first few weeks and months, their feelings will probably keep on changing. One minute they might feel very sad that the way of life they have known for so long is coming to an end. They may want to cry or just be quiet on their own. The next minute they might feel angry with their parents for letting them down. They may feel like shouting, or asking what they have done to deserve all this. Some of the time they might feel lost and frightened, and worried about what will happen to them in the future.

At this early stage, it is common to feel helpless, as if everything is out of control. But it may help to remember that lots of other young people have been through a similar experience. Many of them have found it helpful to talk to someone, perhaps a friend or a relative, who knows them really well. Some people feel better if they write down their feelings or do some drawings. Getting some exercise—going out running or kicking a ball around—can also help you to feel better and less wound up.

▼ *Sometimes talking to a friend can really help. Just getting out and doing something active can make you feel much better.*

"When Mom told me that Dad was leaving, I felt really angry with her. I thought it was all her fault for driving him away. But after I'd calmed down a little I realized that they'd both been unhappy for a long while. I still felt very sad that we couldn't all live together anymore."

Dan, age twelve

I just feel numb

The news that their parents are splitting up can leave the children in the family feeling very numb. For a while they may be just too shocked to experience any emotions at all. Many young people describe the sense of being cut off from everyone around them, even their best friends. For a while they may not be able to concentrate on their schoolwork, or enjoy the activities that they used to find fun. All of these reactions are completely normal and, fortunately, they do not last forever. Eventually, people settle down and begin to enjoy their daily lives again.

Jodie's parents separated when she was nine. Until then she had always enjoyed school, but suddenly she seemed to stop trying. She was rude to her teachers and avoided her friends. One of her teachers was worried about her. She talked to Jodie about the difficult time she was going through, and told Jodie that the same thing had happened to her when she was growing up. After a while Jodie started to find it easier to concentrate on her schoolwork, and began to have fun with her friends again.

◀ *When everything is changing at home, it is hard to concentrate on your schoolwork.*

When you are going through a bad time, it can help to write down your thoughts.

Many young people find it difficult to believe that their parents are really going to separate. They tell themselves that very soon their family will be back together again. But if a couple is determined to split up, it is much better for the children to face up to the situation. Then they can start to travel through their feelings until they gradually begin to feel better again.

Not everyone feels sad when their parents split up. In families where there have been a lot of arguments, the children may be relieved that they no longer have to listen to fights every day. This is a perfectly understandable reaction and children should not feel guilty if this is how they feel.

Is it my fault?

It is very common for young people who are involved in a family breakup to believe that the split is somehow their fault. They wonder if their mom and dad might have stayed together if only they had been better behaved, or asked for less allowance, or simply made their parents happier. But children are not the cause of family breakups. When a couple separates, it is the result of problems between two adults.

All families have arguments between parents and children, especially in the children's teenage years. Even in the happiest families, parents get angry about messy bedrooms or staying out late. But when parents are under stress because they are not getting along well, the fights often increase and become more serious.

▲ When a parent leaves home, the children may blame themselves.

Sometimes a young person might hear parents arguing and notice that his or her name is being mentioned a lot. The child may decide that his or her parents are angry or upset with the child. But in fact the parents are probably just trying to figure out what will be best for their children.

Parents' love for their children is very different from their feelings about each other. Two adults can be disappointed in each other, and fall "out of love." However, if parents have caring relationships with their children these bonds are very hard to break.

▼ *It is perfectly normal for parents to have arguments with their teenage children.*

"In the year before Mom and Dad split up Mom and I had lots of arguments. She was always going on about the mess in my room, and when I asked for new clothes she went nuts. When she moved out I felt really guilty, as if I had driven her away. But she told me later that she and Dad had been fighting all the time, and that was why she was so stressed out with me."
Joel, age fifteen

Talking it over

When families break up, many young people find it very helpful to share their thoughts and feelings with somebody else. They may decide to talk to a relative, such as a grandparent, or they may choose someone outside their family, perhaps a teacher or a counselor. Whomever they choose, it can be very comforting to talk to someone whom they like and trust.

It is also good for young people to talk to their parents about what is going on. Sometimes this can be difficult, especially if everyone is upset, but most parents will want to know what is worrying their children. It's all right to ask questions rather than worry in silence about things like who's going to get the family pet, but you should be prepared for your mom and dad not to have all the answers.

Even if they seem distracted in the middle of a family breakup, your parents will want to know what's worrying you.

Some young people share their feelings with their brothers and sisters, and some talk to their friends. It is surprising how many people have been through a family breakup, and it can be very reassuring to discover that you are not alone. Once you start talking to your friends, you may find out that some of them have experienced the same sort of feelings and worries as you.

▲ *Sharing your feelings with a friend when you are going through a bad time at home can make you feel much better.*

FACT:
In the United States a divorce is completed on average every thirteen seconds of the day. Fewer than half of America's children can expect to spend their entire childhood living with both of their biological parents in the same home.
Divorce Resource Network statistic

5. Splitting Up

Early days

The early stages of splitting up can be very painful and confusing for the whole family. When one parent leaves home, it can feel sad and strange without that parent around. However, if there have been a lot of arguments, it is sometimes a relief for everyone that the quarrels are over. Sometimes the parent who is still at home becomes more relaxed, and daily life can be easier to cope with.

▼ It is great to be able to comfort your parent when he or she is feeling low, but you shouldn't feel it is up to you to solve his or her problems.

Often one or both parents will be sad and angry and their children may see them crying or hear them shouting on the phone. This can be very hard for children to deal with, especially if they are feeling upset themselves. The children may feel that it is up to them to make their mom or dad feel better. However, it is important to realize that adults need to sort their feelings out for themselves. Children should be allowed to get on with enjoying their own lives as much as possible. In the early days

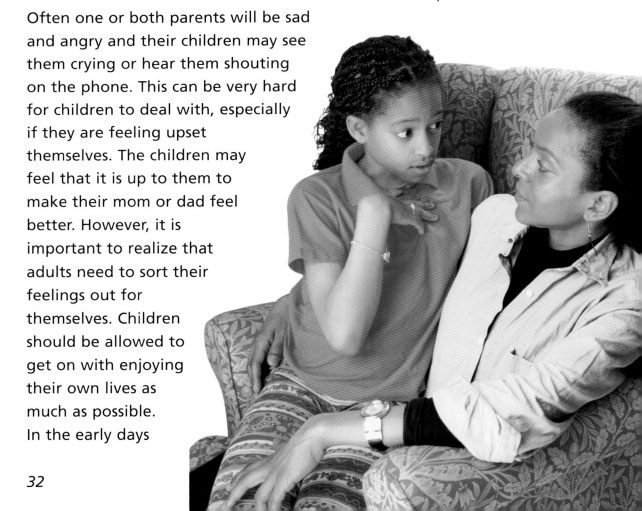

after a split, children often feel very torn between their parents. They may want to take sides and get very angry with their mom or dad. This is a natural reaction, but it is much better for everyone if children don't get involved in their parents' arguments. When children join in an argument it upsets everyone.

In some families the breakup doesn't happen right away. One partner may move out for a short while and then come back again. This can be very unsettling for the children, who don't know whether their parents will end up together or apart.

"The first few weeks after Dad left felt really weird. Mom was crying a lot of the time, and I was trying hard to cheer her up. In the end I realized I couldn't do much to make her feel better. So I went out for the afternoon with my friend and then brought her home with me for supper. Actually, that seemed to cheer Mom up a lot."

Laura, age fourteen

After a divorce, children may need to help more around the house.

Where will I live?

When a family splits up, decisions need to be made about where the children will spend their time.

Some separated parents make arrangements for their children to spend half their time in one parent's house and half in the other's. This works especially well when parents live close to each other so that their children can move easily from one house to the other. In many other separated families, the children spend weekdays with one parent and visit their other parent on the weekends and during the school breaks. But each family is different, and what matters most is that both parents continue to play an important part in their children's lives.

▼ *Some children spend weekdays at their mom's house and visit their dad on the weekends and vacations.*

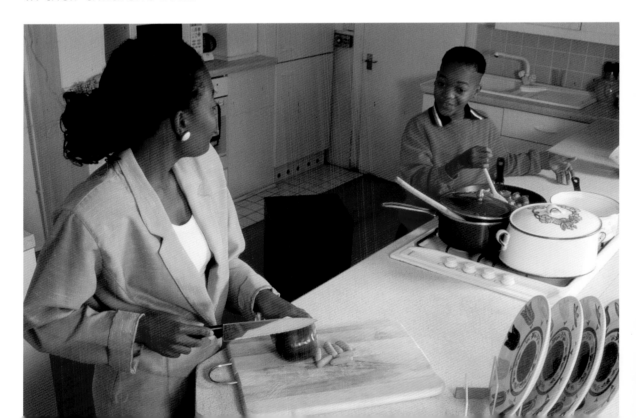

case study • case study • case study • case study • case study

Peter and Lucy live with their dad during the week. He is a designer who works from home, so he can take them to school and look after them in the evenings. Their mom is a nurse who often works nights. They go to stay with her on the weekends and spend a lot of their vacations with her.

Sadly, not all parents manage to agree about where their children should live. Sometimes couples have to go to court so that a judge can decide which parent the children should live with, and when and where they should see the other parent. The judge's job is to make the best arrangements for the children. Whenever possible, this will involve both parents spending some time with their children.

▲ *In some separated families, the father is the parent who looks after the children most of the time.*

A new way of life

It can take a long time to get used to living with just one parent instead of two. Most children miss doing special things with their mom or their dad. After a family breaks up, many single parents move to a smaller house or apartment. Usually both parents have less money to spend than before, so they may need to spend more time at work than they used to.

▲ *Single-parent families generally have less money to spend on food than families with two parents.*

FACT:
During the 1990s the U.S. National Bureau of Economic Research conducted a survey of family incomes before and after divorce. They studied the family income of children whose parents had divorced and remain divorced for at least six years. During this time, the income of the family fell by 40 to 45 percent.

Sometimes single parents can be very tired at the end of the day. They may also need more help around the house. In some cases the children can feel that their mom or dad is just too tired and busy to spend time with them, but sometimes the opposite is true. Many young people find that after their parents split up, they have a chance to get to know their mom and dad really well. Instead of arguing with his or her partner all the time, both parents have more time and energy to do enjoyable things with their children.

Many children don't manage to see as much of both their parents as they would like and, in a few cases, one parent disappears entirely from their lives. When this happens, it is natural for children to feel very sad and to miss that parent.

▼ *Some separated parents find they have more time to spend having fun with their children.*

Seeing both parents

Many young people live with one parent but visit the other one regularly. This arrangement can work very well, but there can also be problems. Sometimes young people feel disappointed that they are not in the place they want to be. Perhaps there is a party close to their mom's house while they are away for the weekend with their dad. In situations like this, it is good for the children to tell their parents how they feel. Sometimes it might be possible to rearrange the dates of a visit. However, many young people decide that it is worth giving up a few parties in order to spend some time with their other parent.

Sometimes one parent will give the children lots of expensive presents and treats. This is a way of showing love for the children, but it can be very hard for the other parent to watch this happening, especially if he or she does not have a lot of money to spend on the children. He or she may start to feel jealous and angry that he or she cannot give the children treats, too.

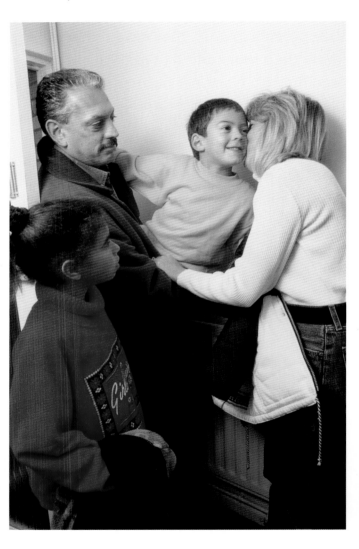

▲ *For many children, switching between two houses is just a normal part of life.*

Many separated parents manage to cooperate very well together. But, sadly, there are cases where the children feel that they are caught in the middle of their parents' arguments. Sometimes parents complain to their children about the things the other parent does. They may ask questions about their ex-partner's life and even suggest that the children pass on messages. This can be very upsetting for the children involved. lYoung people should never be expected to take sides in their parents' arguments.

FACT:
In 1991 about 20 million children in the United States lived with just one parent. This is 28 percent of all U.S. children. Of these, the vast majority (84 percent) lived with their mother.

◀ It is great to have fun with your dad, especially if you don't see him very much because he is separated from your mom. However, sometimes there can be problems over too many presents or treats.

New partners

After a couple has been apart for a while, one or both of them may find a new partner. This can be difficult for their children to cope with. Although the children may be happy that their mom or dad has found someone new, they will probably also feel sad, because there is now very little chance that their parents will ever get back together again.

Jon and his mom had been living on their own for a year when she met Paul. At first Jon was angry about Paul. Jon was the one who looked after his mom now and they didn't need anyone else in their life. Jon also didn't like it when Paul told him when it was time to go to bed. Jon talked to his mom about his feelings, and Paul stopped telling him what to do. They started playing football and computer games together and Jon decided it was fun having Paul around.

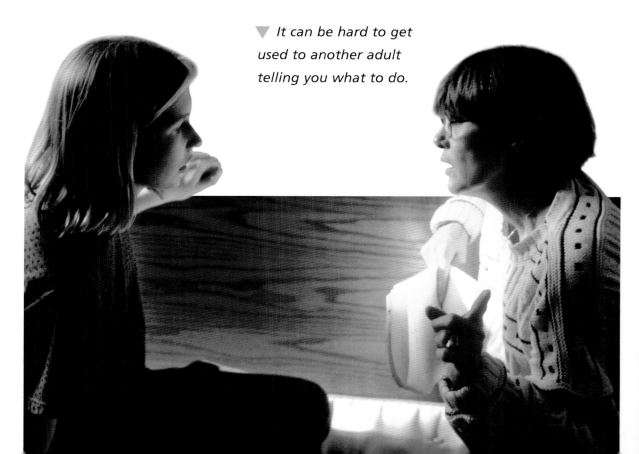

▼ *It can be hard to get used to another adult telling you what to do.*

It can be hard to get used to having another adult in your life. In particular many young people resent it when someone who is not their parent tells them what to do. In these situations, it is a good idea for children to talk to their mom or dad and tell them what's making them unhappy.

Sometimes it just takes time to get used to a parent's new partner. But after a while, young people may find that they like having the new man or woman around. Of course they know that the new partner will never replace their real mom or dad, but they can still enjoy being together.

▲ *Eventually you may start to enjoy having your parent's new partner around.*

6. Moving On

Looking ahead

Although there are many things that take a long time to adjust to, there comes a time when separated families begin to settle down into their new way of life. Parents become less upset and angry and children get used to their new routines.

Eventually one or both parents might marry again and there may be stepbrothers and stepsisters to get to know. This can be a big challenge for all the children involved. It can be very hard to get along with other children, and to share your mom or dad with someone else.

▲ *Some stepfamilies work really well, and everyone has fun and enjoys being with one another.*

Sometimes, stepbrothers and stepsisters never really get along well, and nobody should feel guilty about this. However, some stepfamilies work very well, and the young people have a lot of good times together.

Many young people will have a new half brother or half sister, if their mom or dad has a baby with a new partner. This can be a very exciting time, but it is also possible to feel left out. It's good to talk to your family about how you are feeling about the new baby.

Whatever happens in your family, there will be new challenges to face. After a while you will stop looking back and thinking so much about the past, and start to think about the future instead.

"We met Sarah and her boys when Mom and Dad had been divorced for two years. We usually saw them for part of the weekend when we were visiting Dad. We got along really well with the boys and at first I thought that Sarah was just a family friend. When I realized that she was Dad's girlfriend, I was really pleased. Now Dad and Sarah have been married for five years, and all of us kids get along really well together."

Alex, age thirteen

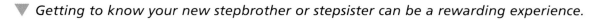

▼ *Getting to know your new stepbrother or stepsister can be a rewarding experience.*

Feeling better now

As time passes, things usually get much easier for everyone in the family. Most young people stop feeling so sad and start having fun with their friends again.

However, although daily life definitely gets better, there can be times when it feels bad again. On special occasions such as birthdays and holidays, it can feel sad not to have both parents together. Family vacations with just one parent can seem strange. There are also stages in young people's lives when they really miss having their other parent around. For example, as they reach puberty, they may wish that they could talk to a parent of the same sex about the changes they are going through.

◄ It's great to have your mom around to give you advice, and if she is not there, it is only natural that you will miss her.

Or perhaps, if there is a problem in their life, they will miss being able to talk to a parent who "would have known exactly what to say."

But despite these difficult times, many young people look back on their family breakup and realize that it may have been the best thing for everyone. They recognize that their parents were very unhappy together and that they couldn't continue to live as they were. Of course some children of separated parents may always feel sad that their parents had to part, but, as time passes, they will probably be able to feel much calmer about it.

"Being with Mom and Dad now, I can tell that they are both much happier than they were two years ago. It's been very hard living through the divorce, but I think we're all looking forward to the future now."

Kate, age fourteen

▼ Once everything has settled down after a family breakup, it feels good to relax and enjoy life again, perhaps with a new step-parent as part of the family.

GLOSSARY

abuse
to treat a person cruelly, either physically, verbally, or both

addicted
unable to give up something, such as alcohol, tobacco, or drugs

adjust
get used to something

bankrupt
having no money, unable to pay debts

communication
sharing thoughts and feelings, talking to other people

concentrate
to focus your thoughts closely on something, such as work or a book

cooperate
to work together with someone else

counselor
someone who has been trained to listen to other people's problems and who tries to give good advice to help them

criticize
to tell someone what is wrong with them or what they have done wrong

divorce
official, legal ending of a marriage

emotions
strong feelings, such as happiness, love, sadness, anger

half brother/sister
siblings who share only one parent. For example, two brothers may have the same mother but different fathers.

nuclear family
family where the parents and their children all live together

numb
unable to feel anything

puberty
time, normally during early teenage years, when a person's body changes from a child's to an adult's

social worker
professional who helps provide services to those in need of financial or emotional support. Social workers can themselves be counselors, or they can help people find counselors or other needed services.

spouse
husband or wife

stepbrother/sister
son or daughter of one's mother or father's new spouse

stepfamily
family of one's mother or father's new spouse

sympathetic
understanding about someone else's troubles

BOOKS TO READ

Armitage, Ronda. *Family Violence.* Chicago: Raintree, 2000.

Bishop, Keeley, and Penny Tripp. *Family Breakup.* Chicago: Heinemann, 2003.

MacGregor, Cynthia. *The Divorce Helpbook for Kids.* Atascadero, Calif.: Impact, 2001.

Wagner, Heather Lehr. *Understanding and Coping with Divorce.* Broomall, Penn.: Chelsea House, 2002.

GETTING ADVICE

There are many different websites and organizations that can give you information about divorce, and advice on how to deal with your parents' divorce. These organizations vary from state to state. Here are some good ways to locate help:
• Talk to your school counselor or teacher.
• Ask a school or public librarian for a list of resources in your area.
• Use a kid friendly search engine like www.yahooligans.com to do an online search. Try looking up the words "divorce," "help," and "kids."
• Look in your local phone book for hotlines.

INDEX

Numbers in **bold** refer to pages with pictures.

abuse **21**
addiction 20
alcohol **20**, 21
anger 24, 25, 38, 42
arguments **12, 13,** 17, 27, 28, 32, 33, 37, 39
Australia 5

babies, new **19**, 43
bankruptcy 16
birthdays 44

Childline 21
children 13, **19**, 21, 22, 23, 24, 26, 27, 28, 29, 30, 32, 33, 34, 35, 36, 37, 38, 39, 40, 42
Christmas 44
comforting parents **32**, 33
communication 7, 14, 15, 22, **23, 25,** 30, 31
cooperation 39
coping methods 14
counseling **22, 23**
counselors 20, **22**, 23, 30
courts 35
criticism 13

death in family 16, **17**
divorce 4, 5, 11, 21, 33, 36, 43, 45
divorce, effect on family income 36
divorce rates 5, 31
drinking problems **20**, 21
drug addiction 20

emotions when a family splits up **24**, 25, **26**, 27, 32, 33, 37
family, death in **17**
family, having fun as a **8**
financial problems 16, 36

friends, talking to **24, 25,** 30, **31**

guilt, feelings of 27, **28**, 29

half brother 43
half sister 43

illness 16, 17
individual pursuits 7

jealousy 38
jobs, losing **16**

living with one parent 33, **34, 35, 36, 37,** 38, 39, 44

marriage **4, 5,** 6, 10, 11, **15,** 42
missing a parent 36, 37, 44, **44,** 45
money worries 12, 16, 19, 36, **36**
moving 9, 16, **18,** 19, 36

nuclear families 5

parent leaving home **28,** 32, 33
partners, new **40, 41**
problems in family 16
puberty 44

redundancy 16
refuges **21**
remarriage 42
resentment, feelings of 41

sadness **24,** 32
schoolwork **26**
shock **26**
single-parent families 36, **37,** 39
social workers 20

splitting up 10, 11, 12, 13, 15, 21, 24, 26, 27, 28, 32, 33
stepbrother 42, **43**
stepfamilies 42, 43, **45**
stepsister 42, **43**
stress **9,** 19, 28, **29**

taking sides 33, 39
talking to friends **24, 25,** 30, **31**
teachers 21, 26, 30
treats 38, **39**

United Kingdom 5, 21
United States 5, 31, 39
U.S. National Bureau of Economic Research 36

violence, domestic 20, **21**
visiting a parent 34, 38

young couples **11**